UNOFFICIAL GUIDE TO
Michigan Zoos

Mitten Publishing LLC
www.mittenpublishing.com

Michigan Map of Zoos

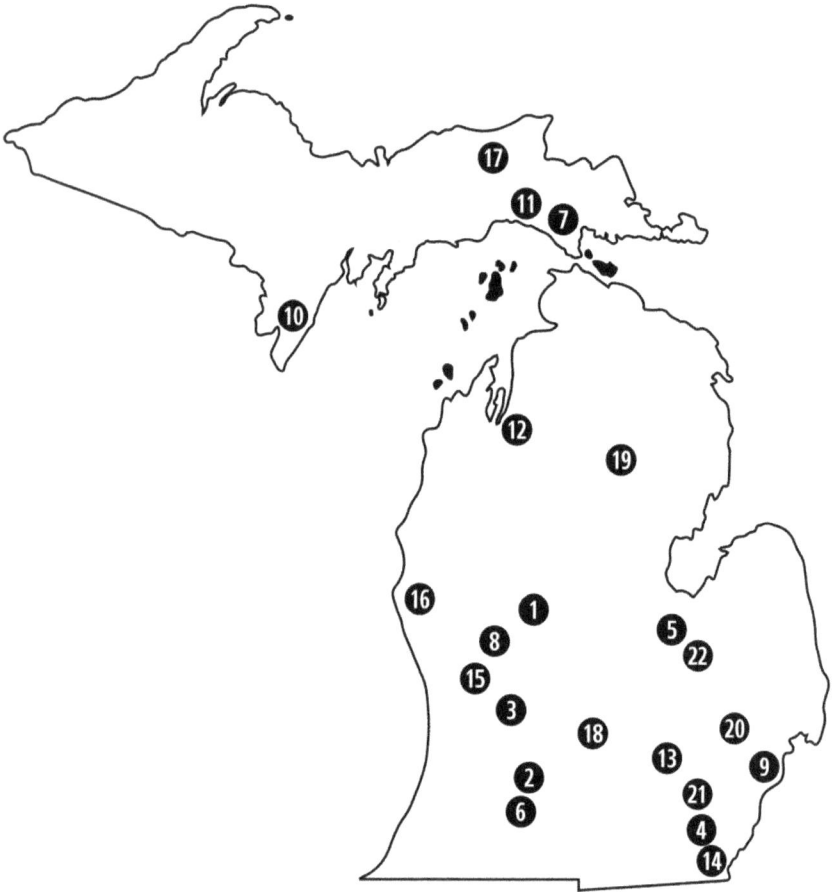

UNOFFICIAL GUIDE TO

Michigan Zoos

by
Timothy Payne

First Edition

Mitten Publishing LLC
PO Box 605
Concord, Michigan 49237

Unless stated otherwise, all content is a collection of recollections and experiences by the author. All parks were visited and toured in person. No ghost writing in this book! Content is for entertainment purposes and does not constitute professional travel advice.

The author accepts no responsibility for the content or accuracy of information on third party websites.

We are all only human and tend to make a grammatical or spelling error from time to time that even our best editors and proofreaders may miss. Please share any such mishaps via email to tim@mittenpublishing.com

First Edition: July 6, 2019
Printed in the United States of America
ISBN: 978-1-7338916-0-8

To Aunt Jean…my high school English teacher that gave me a way to dig out of a failing grade while being sneaky at getting me to improve my writing skills. Thank you for the A's I "earned" in your class. Thank you for this unique life skill. Thank you for being one of my coolest teachers.

Table of Contents

Preface

I live within a 45-minute drive from two major zoos in mid-Michigan. I have visited, and even ran through one as part of a 5K running and walking event.

One thing I have learned is that not all zoos are created equal. However, they all have one or two things that make them stand out and worthy of a visit or revisit. I am writing this book based on my experiences and adventures at these various establishments.

I will be describing all of these cool and unique places to you in alphabetical order by property name. Use the map on the next page to visualize where each zoo is located in relationship to my chapter about it.

Although this is not an official travel guide, nor written by a travel guide professional, please feel free to use it to help plan your very own zoo adventures. Try a zoomarathon if you have the gumption. "Zoomarathon" is a word I created when planning to visit two or more zoos in one day or weekend.

Enjoy!

UNOFFICIAL GUIDE TO
Michigan Zoos

❶ Anderson & Girls Orchard

TOWN:

Stanton

DESCRIPTION AND EXPERIENCE

I thought I would start this book about Michigan zoos by describing my experience at an Orchard. Originally this chapter was not going to make it into this book because it did not show up in any of my initial research on Michigan zoos. Then a good friend and book author, Ron Rademacher, asked me if I planned to visit Anderson & Girls Orchard. So later that day, I did a little more research, sent an email or two, and here it is!

Anderson & Girls Orchard was established in 1978 when Terry Anderson, who at that time worked at the orchard, purchased it from Orville Trebian. However, it was not until about the year 2000 when they added five goats and two jersey calves that it really started attracting visitors. From then on, more animals have found their way to calling this orchard their home, including three different species of camel.

My visit happened to be just a couple of days after their season opened in late March, which was a week before their normally advertised season. This was good luck for me, as I was originally planning to visit later in May. Since this was opening weekend and the winter here had ended harshly, I decided to splurge for a private tour to satisfy my case of stir-craziness. Please note that being a regular guest here is pretty cool on its own, but getting a private tour...well, that is another kind of awesome experience!

For a spring day, I was met with chilly temperatures that reminded me that I could not put away my winter coat and boots just yet. My tour started by visiting their petting zoo of goats and donkey. Another interesting inhabitant nearby in his own pen was a spirited zeedonk, which is a cross between a zebra and a donkey.

Many of the inhabitants here have been domesticated or trained by the handlers in order to provide a safe and caring environment for everyone. Their menagerie of camels is a good example of domesticated animals. They all were very friendly and demanded attention from our tour guide. I was even able to feed them each an apple. They are very tall but graceful.

Please be warned that though many zoo animals have been handled since they were very young, this does not mean it is safe for you to just start petting them. A tip for success is to ask a handler if it is okay to touch or pet a normally wild creature.

In total, there are many different species of animals here at the orchard worth taking the time to see. From amphibians and lizards, a tortoise and hare run (so to speak), birds and primates, wallaby and kangaroo, as well as a number of reindeer and other regular barnyard animals. There are many outdoor enclosures as well as indoor ones. There are bobcats and other carnivorous inhabitants here to enjoy, as well as a boisterous Eurasian eagle owl.

DAYS AND HOURS OF OPERATION

Anderson & Girls Orchard is open to the public beginning in April through the first of December. Check out their website for details.

MUST SEE

Many zoos across the state feature a walk-through parakeet enclosure. This is actually a great way for people to interact with and take really cool pictures and selfies with them. You can purchase food that will invite these colorful birds to land on your hands, arms, shoulders, and sometimes your head to partake of this treat of seeds.

Another opportunity to interact with some of the animals is to feed and pet the goats in what I think is the coolest enclosure of all. If you do not know it already, goats love to climb. The enclosure here encourages these goats to climb up way above your head for an interesting view and awesome photographic opportunity. There is even a uniquely-designed mechanism where you can transport treats all the way to the top platform. This will help entice the goats to venture up there.

This property is also a working orchard where you can get all your apple-based products and donuts anytime during their season. You can even come out and pick your own strawberries during season.

They have an impressive two-story gift shop, since it caters to zoo life AND the orchard. A recent addition is an ice cream shop. Though it was a little chilly outside for me, I can never say "no" to ice cream.

FIELD NOTES

Whenever I start a sentence with the word, "So" it means that I am about to say something that I feel is fairly important. So, this one day...before visiting the Anderson & Girls Orchard, I decided to purchase their private tour package...

SPECIAL AUTHOR NOTE: Before I go any further, I want to recommend that if your budget allows for a private tour at any of the properties that offer them...it is money well spent. I did splurge on a couple of private tours during my research for this book. Unfortunately, I had to limit these due to my shoestring budget (meaning I did not have a lot of money). However, I do plan to return to all properties a number of times over the next few years and will enhance my educational experiences as I can. I am also certain I will have many more stories because of it.

A private tour will immerse you in an awesome educational experience as well as pose the opportunity to interact with some unique inhabitants. This will most likely depend upon a number of factors including time of visit, tour guide, temperature, and any number of reasons.

While here, I was invited to feed mini marshmallows to a pair of common marmosets (very small monkeys). Once I held still, they came down and took the treat from my hand and then quickly scampered away to eat them. In time, they seemed to get more comfortable with me in their enclosure and were quicker in coming to get their second marshmallow.

My most memorable encounter was with a pair of coatimundi. My guide was telling me that she raised them from babies (called kittens) and they were very docile. They are very curious, just like their cousin, the raccoon. At one point when we were talking, one of them jumped onto my shoulders and started sniffing around and in the hood of my coat. At first I thought, "Oh great, what do I do now?" Well, the answer was simple in this case...enjoy the experience! I was able to pet his back and long tail. I even got a couple pictures taken of us before he jumped back to their ledge. The female coatimundi was a bit shyer, but she warmed up to me before I left the enclosure.

Please keep in mind that I have only described a few encounters. A private tour will cover much more than what you read here.

Final Field Note...visit often and ask questions. Lots of questions. Anderson & Girls Orchard seems to grow continuously with different types of animals. They have acquired and shared a number of animals with other Michigan zoos. Ask them about their various animal exchanges. Ask about the pair of grey wolves that they had once acquired, why they are no longer at the orchard, and where they live now.

CONTACT INFORMATION

Anderson & Girls Orchard
2985 N Sheridan Road
Stanton, MI 48888
(989) 831-4228
Website:
http://www.andersonandgirls.com/
andergirls@hotmail.com

❷ Binder Park Zoo

TOWN

Battle Creek

DESCRIPTION AND EXPERIENCE

I have been to this zoo a number of times, since it is the closest park to where I live. We have taken our children here as well as chaperoned school field trips. I even ran a 5K race here with my daughter and friends called the "Cheetah Chase."

Binder Park Zoo was founded in 1977 on a 433-acre plot. It is one of the largest zoos in Michigan. They offer a number of unique opportunities and camps throughout the season to provide a great educational setting.

When I visited, this was the second property for the day of my zoomarathon. I parked at around 2 p.m. on a mid-September day. The coolness of the day helped provide a great observatory advantage over the warmer summer days. The Mexican grey wolves were very active, and they seemed to be interested in activity near one side of their enclosure. At first, I thought it was their handlers, but I did not see anyone. I did notice movement outside of the habitat. It appeared to be a rabbit. I believe the rabbit was safe at all times, but the wolves' interest surely made them active and fun to observe.

There are several enclosures that feature viewing panes or windows. This technology has improved over the years and it made viewing the inhabitants very pleasant. They allowed me to capture a few nice pictures through the glass with my camera.

DAYS OF OPERATION

Binder Park Zoo is open to the public between mid-April through the first week of October. You can easily create a small zoomarathon between this park and Critchlow Alligator Sanctuary which is only about a twenty-minute drive away. This is what I did, and it worked out very well.

MUST SEE

Take the free tram ride or walk from the main zoo area to Wild Africa. This area of the park offers another nice walking tour, as you start in an African village and wind your way through many exhibits.

If you want an interesting giraffe encounter, this is the place to visit. Zoo guests will stand just about face-to-face with these fantastically tall herbivores. I suggest purchasing treats from the zoo staff for feeding the giraffe. You might be amazed at just how long their tongues are.

Since it was later in the afternoon when I got to Wild Africa, there were only a couple giraffes interested in being fed. However, I did get a nice picture of a number of them walking up the far hillside where their lodging sets.

There are number of other animals that roam the range with the giraffes. You can view them all from different areas including the African village. When talking to one of the staff members, I asked if there had been any successful breeding programs here. In response to that, he pointed to the far left from where we stood where a zebra mare was nursing her foal that was born only a few weeks earlier. From where I was standing, they were slightly obscured by foliage.

In a neighboring exhibit, three cheetahs were very active. I am not sure what had their attention, but it was nice seeing these large cats much closer than in my other visits. Their walking around made them great candidates for some amateur photography with the right camera...not mine, however.

Continuing my walk, there is a nice wooded area, which almost seems like it is not even in the park. What came to mind is that there is plenty of space for potential expansion in the future.

FIELD NOTES

Take a walk through the Swamp Adventure. Get an up-close and personal experience with one of Michigan's natural beauties...marshland. This path is all boardwalk and keeps you just above the water line. Notice the sounds, smells, plant and animal life in this area. This is Michigan nature at its best.

On my way back through this large loop I walked next to a family of trumpeter swan. From my research about this species of swan, these three youngsters were actually two years old since they had white feathers instead of grey. Young swan are called cygnets, while adolescent swan are called subadults. There was a natural fence of vegetation between us, so we were not threatening to each other.

There are a number of exhibits that have zoo staff close at hand. When you see these staff members, take advantage of the opportunity to ask questions about the animals. You will find they are quite knowledgeable and love to share information and stories.

CONTACT INFORMATION

Binder Park Zoo
7400 Division Dr
Battle Creek, MI 49014
(269) 979-1351
Website: http://www.binderparkzoo.org/
info@binderparkzoo.org

ZOO AFFILIATIONS & SPONSORSHIPS

Association of Zoos & Aquariums (AZA)

A note about the Association of Zoos & Aquarium accreditation process as shared to me by the CEO of Binder Park Zoo. Accreditation by the AZA is a process that is evaluated by a panel of twelve experts. The standards of the AZA pertain to animal management and care. The accreditation is good for five years. However, the process of completing the application can take almost a full year.

❸ Boulder Ridge Wild Animal Park

TOWN

Alto (about 20 miles east of Grand Rapids)

DESCRIPTION AND EXPERIENCE

The first thing that struck me as unique with this park was the fact that it is set way out in Michigan country. Quite a difference compared to the urban parks around the state. I was in Grand Rapids on a business trip just north of the park. The GPS (Global Positioning System) on the phone was helpful on this.

This 80-acre plot is home to both groomed and wooded areas. The owners originally kept their zoo husbandry operation a secret from the public for about 20 years; that was until an acquaintance of theirs convinced them to turn the property into a zoo. It opened to the public in 2011.

The exhibits are laid out fairly close to one another, but it appears that inhabitants all have plenty of room to stretch their legs, wings, or whatever they need to stretch.

When I entered the park, I literally walked into a live presentation with their Eurasian eagle owl. This magnificent bird taught us onlookers how large our eyes would have to be in comparison to theirs. We also heard silent wings flapping as he flew from post to post during the demonstration. The zookeeper shared a lot of knowledge about this owl species and then allowed guests to come up to the owl to take pictures.

MUST SEE

Included in the cost of admission, you can take a safari trip on one of their rather uniquely modified buses. As you listen to the pre-recorded narration, you will get the best story on the history of the park. The driver will stop the bus often so guests can stand up and get a better look at the animals or take pictures. I found this to be one of the best features of the park.

The parakeet enclosure allows you to get up close and personal with hundreds of these brightly feathered birds. I am not sure how many birds were in the aviary, but it was rather noisy from all their chatter. For a small fee you can feed the parakeets, and they are not shy about landing on your hand to enjoy your offering of seeds.

DAYS AND HOURS OF OPERATION

Boulder Ridge Wild Animal Park is open from late April through the middle of October. Opening time is at 10 a.m. each day except Sunday, when the animals get to sleep in a couple of hours.

FIELD NOTES

I was most impressed by the number of animals born in the park during the year of this book's writing. These newborns included a giraffe, birds of many feathers, and a number of kangaroos. The joeys appeared to be outgrowing their pouches when I saw them. One kangaroo mother had a huge joey leg sticking out of her pouch; it looked like a foot hanging over the side of a warm and furry hammock.

Depending on the time of the year you visit, observe the kangaroo and see how many babies you can find. Then, locate a zookeeper and ask them how many joey's there really are.

So, if you are into photography, I suggest taking the safari trip at least twice. Be sure to ride on both sides of the bus to better your chance at seeing all the animals. This is a great way of creating additional opportunities for that one fantastic animal photograph.

CONTACT INFORMATION

Boulder Ridge Wild Animal Park
8313 Pratt Lake Ave SE
Alto, MI 49302
(616) 868-6711
Website: www.boulderridgewap.com/
info@boulderridgewap.com

ZOO AFFILIATIONS & SPONSORSHIPS

Zoological Association of America (ZAA)

The Zoological Association of America promotes responsible ownership, management, conservation, and propagation of animals in both privately funded and publicly funded facilities through professional standards in husbandry, animal care, safety and ethics. Members that have met these requirements are granted accreditation.

Zoo Tip:

Look for encounter schedules and follow them.

❹ Cabela's Outfitters

TOWN

Dundee

DESCRIPTION AND EXPERIENCE

Until the year 2000, Dundee was little more than a name on an exit sign off Hwy 23 about twenty miles north of the state line from Ohio. Once Cabela's opened, it placed Dundee on the map of popular tourist attractions.

Most people stop there to look at and purchase items that cater to many out-of-door activities such as boating, fishing, hunting, and camping.

So, why the heck did I include this place in a book about zoos? To start with, it houses a fascinating collection of animal specimens from around the world, but mostly from North America. These animals have been preserved through an art called "taxidermy" and are not much different from what

21

you would see in New York City's Museum of Natural History.

Inside the Dundee store you will find an actual mountain of North American animals depicting many scenes of serenity and beauty. You will also see glimpses of predator and prey interaction throughout the mountain and all around the store. Take the time to read the plaques. They spell out the various species names. Look in every nook and cranny of this store, as there are individual animals all over, as well as a few hidden animal scenes.

They also have a large aquarium that houses many live fish found in Michigan waters. The water was crystal clear, making it possible to capture a selfie or two without too much glare.

Please note that every Cabela's has a unique statue in the front of the building. The primary display and scenes are different at each location as well.

MUST SEE

Look for the African exhibit. There you will see some photos next to certain animals. Notice the year, and then think about how well these animals are preserved. It is amazing how well these animals look and how natural they are posed.

DAYS AND HOURS OF OPERATION

Cabela's Outfitters is open daily during their regular store hours.

FIELD NOTES

As of this writing, I had sent an email suggesting they place informational placards that describe the animal, its native habitat, and where it is listed on an endangered species listing. Their response thanked me for the suggestion but did not say if this was something they would contemplate doing.

I think having printed or digital signage may help bring a positive educational element to this type of conservation. I would love to know more about taxidermy and how they determined some of the poses and scenes that are scattered throughout the store.

CONTACT INFORMATION

Cabela's Dundee
110 Cabelas Blvd E
Dundee, MI 48131
(734) 529-4700
Website:
https://www.cabelas.com/stores/Michigan/Dun
dee/

❺ Saginaw Children's Zoo

TOWN

Saginaw

DESCRIPTION AND EXPERIENCE

A series of thunderstorms blanketed most of mid-Michigan when I left the house for the Saginaw Children's Zoo (formerly called Children's Zoo at Celebration Square). The ride was interesting as well since Google Maps was not aware a couple of roads on my route being closed due to major reconstruction. The plus side to the minor delay was that the rain stopped and most of the ground water had dried up, making it a rather enjoyable start to my Saturday morning at the park.

The first area I went into included a number of North American birds. I got my first close up look at a red-tailed hawk, which was a nice change from the hundreds I see high up in the sky or trees. There were also a couple of Mexican gray wolves running around a spacious enclosure. It was nice seeing they had plenty of room and a couple of well-placed observation locations for us humans.

I was surprised to find the bald eagle exhibit had no fencing or netting. This was the first zoo I had been to that did not surround the enclosure with netting of some kind. The opportunity this provided was an unfettered look at a pair of these magnificent birds. One was bathing itself in a plastic storage tote, which gave me a great view of its huge wingspan as it flapped its wings to dry off. Unfortunately, I was not quick enough with my camera to capture it.

The prairie dog exhibit was fun to watch as they were all out repairing their dens from the morning rain showers. I noticed that there were a few kits playing in the mud and they seemed to be really enjoying themselves. The prairie dogs here were my first sign of successful animal husbandry. Animal husbandry is the science that encourages wild animal breeding in captivity.

There was also an enclosure that the public can enter, that has you go through a double set of gates.

Once inside, I was able to get close to some kangaroos, wallabies, and an emu. It really made for a great personal experience as well as a fantastic photo opportunity without fencing in the way. I asked the zookeeper if they had many successful births in the park other than the prairie dogs. She responded that they did not have many during the year I wrote this, but she was excited that there might be baby penguins in the coming year. With luck, visitors will be able to see a homegrown crèche (a group of baby penguins) in the spring.

DAYS AND HOURS OF OPERATION

The Saginaw Children's Zoo opens in the later part of April through early October. They are open on specific dates in October and November, though all animals may not be on exhibit.

MUST SEE

So, this might not be animal related, but the experience was fun. In the middle of the property is this large pond. In this pond, there are at least three different species of lily pads growing. They were bright with blooms when I was there. Anyway, at one end is a path of large stones that lead to a wooden bridge. Walk across the bridge for an interesting and unique experience. I double-dog-dare you.

FIELD NOTES

There is a path/ramp that takes you into a typical Michigan pond. Check it out as it is full of many fun facts about freshwater fish as well as those living in the pond. You might even see some of them swimming about. There are many cabinets and drawers to explore as well for additional education on Michigan animals.

CONTACT INFORMATION

Saginaw Children's Zoo
2876, 1730 S Washington Ave.
Saginaw, MI 48601
(989) 759-1408
Website: https://www.saginawzoo.com/

ZOO AFFILIATIONS & SPONSORSHIPS

Association of Zoos & Aquariums (AZA)

❻ Critchlow Alligator Sanctuary

TOWN

Athens

DESCRIPTION AND EXPERIENCE

In 2007, David Critchlow purchased a small piece of land to develop into the alligator sanctuary that we have today. He plays multiple heroic roles, as his investment was a way to retire from his job and to spend time with his wife and family. The property covers just about three acres.

Pulling into the parking lot early on a Sunday morning, we had no idea what to expect. There was a family from out of town waiting for the park to open. Based on their clothing, it was easy to deduce that these visitors were hard-core Cubs fans. Peeking at their license plate they were from out-of-state. Personally, I love seeing non-Michiganders taking advantage of our tourism resources.

The morning was sunny but in the low 70s. It was very comfortable. When we paid admission, we were given the option to walk around on our own or join in on a guided tour. Best tip for a successful experience...do the guided tour on your first visit.

Our group was led by a young woman by the name of Alexis Wood-Pennock. She had worked at the park for about four years. She was very knowledgeable about the park and its inhabitants. We learned all about the types of alligators, ages, reasons for being rescued, as well as their habits and traits.

The tour started with the younger alligators and progressed up to their largest resident. After telling us about each grouping or area, we were invited to feed the alligators the specialized food we purchased with admission.

The guided tour did take a couple of hours to complete and we did spend more time after the tour to revisit some of our new friends and to hand out the rest of the food. It was fascinating to see how they eat.

One area of interest she showed us were the shipping containers where the alligators stay during the cold winter months. These containers are heated to about sixty-five degrees Fahrenheit. Alligators have a form of hibernation called "brumation." They brumate in cooler temperature environments. This makes them less aggressive. They survive during this period by living off the fat stored in their tail.

After the tour, I got a personal animal encounter. I paid for this extra feature with admission and got to hold a small three-year old alligator. He was very docile, and the young woman handling it told me some interesting facts about this specific specimen. I got to feel its nose and around its eyes and teeth. Luckily, its mouth was taped closed with electricians' tape so it could not bite. Rest assured that this does not harm the alligator in any way, and it allows for safe handling.

DAYS AND HOURS OF OPERATION

The Critchlow Alligator Sanctuary is open from mid-April until the Fall Roundup in mid-October. Then weekends only during the winter months.

MUST SEE

Look for the rescued turtles and tortoises.

See Spot run during the guided tour.

The animal encounter was memorable. I had never handled an alligator before. They also have options to handle a snake or a larger (four-foot) alligator.

So, if you want a huge alligator encounter, stop by the park in later October for the Fall Roundup. Your price of admission includes helping the handlers physically transport the alligators from their summer enclosures to the shipping containers located all over the park. I participated in the 2018 Roundup and can tell you firsthand that this was an awesome experience. Mr. Critchlow took one of the smaller alligators and let the younger children learn how to handle them. I doubt anyone left disappointed. As I write this, my muscles are still sore from holding tightly onto a larger gator that wanted to wiggle a lot. From the sounds he made, I do not think he was very happy being manhandled.

During the summer, the park offers a number of Twilight Tours where you can see the alligators at night. The pools look alive with shimmering diamonds that can be captured on camera.

FIELD NOTES

Unintentional breeding program in summer of 2018 - Critchlow Alligator Sanctuary inadvertently positioned itself to host the first alligator breeding in the state of Michigan. For alligators to mate, there have to be special conditions in their environment. No, we are not talking about a candle-lit dinner and romantic music. 2018 was the year Michigan experienced multiple days in the mid-90s. The heat was that "special condition" I was talking about.

The gestation period for alligator eggs are about sixty-five days in the wild. Mr. Critchlow and his staff retrieved about 150 eggs from the soil while other handlers kept the females at a safe distance.

A local snake breeder was invited to try incubating some of the eggs just to see if any would hatch. In the spring of 2019, it was announced on the sanctuary Facebook page that Stubby and Tom were the proud parents to Tubbs. Tubbs may be the only "Michigator" to date, and currently resides in the main building at the park entrance with a couple of other rescue alligators of about the same age.

CONTACT INFORMATION

Critchlow Alligator Sanctuary
1698 M-66
Athens, MI 49011
Owner: David Critchlow
(269) 729-4802
Website: http://peter1671.wixsite.com/cas2018
info@alligatorsanctuary.com

❼ Deer Ranch

TOWN

St. Ignace

DESCRIPTION AND EXPERIENCE

This park opened to the public in 1950 and has been a popular tourist stop since. It does make a beautiful place to take a break and stretch your legs after a long drive getting to the Upper Peninsula or heading back to where we trolls live (Yoopers will get that joke).

The tour starts at the fawn barn where you might get to see some of the newborn whitetails. When I visited the Deer Ranch, there was two light-colored fawn sleeping. I later found out that they will turn white as they get older.

Walking down the path, I did not initially see many deer, for good reason however...it was after 2 p.m. and was rather warm outside. They were in the trees enjoying some shade. Once I started peering into the lightly wooded lots, many deer seemed to materialize before me.

A few bucks even walked out to greet me. Probably because they thought I might have a treat or two for them. As luck would have it, I did have some carrot sticks I had purchased upon entry to the park! If you get a chance, pet their muzzle and nose as you feed them. They are very soft.

In another enclosure there were some doe and their babies. They did not have as many trees for shade, but the turnips that were planted had large leaves that provided them with a cool place to lay. One doe was particularly rambunctious and having a good time as she pranced and ran around the enclosure. It was fun seeing this highly spirited doe run back and forth.

DAYS AND HOURS OF OPERATION

The Deer Ranch is open seven days a week from mid-May through mid-October.

MUST SEE

When you pay for admission, you have a chance to purchase a couple types of food to feed the deer on your adventure. When I asked what their favorite food is, I was told they are particularly fond of apples. However, I decided on a cup of carrot sticks to extend my feeding opportunities. Carrots seemed to be popular that day as well.

FIELD NOTES

Look for the white deer. They are not albino as you might think. The white species of whitetail deer are more rare than albino deer, but can be found in abundance here. Pretty neat that they have been successfully breeding this unique form of whitetail deer for many years.

The turnips I mentioned earlier have a secondary job besides providing shade with their broad leaves. Deer eat the turnips as part of their diet. Ask the staff if there are any deer that favor this plant over apples or carrots.

CONTACT INFORMATION

Deer Ranch
W1540 West US 2
Saint Ignace, MI 49781
Owners: Cullip Family
(906) 643-7760
Website: http://www.deerranch.com/
info@deerranch.com

❽ Deer Tracks Junction

TOWN

Cedar Springs

DESCRIPTION AND EXPERIENCE

I decided to mix up my research to include some holiday and winter visits in order to provide some unique perspectives. Deer Tracks Junction offers a nice holiday tour called the Christmas Experience.

Technically, Deer Tracks Junction is not a zoo, but rather a working farm. It is a "hands-on" farm owned by Kelly Powell and run by his family, where guests have the opportunity to interact with many of the herbivorous inhabitants. They breed and raise these animals for sale while offering the chance to educate guests in this hands-on environment.

The holiday excursion is by appointment only through online registration. The process was easy enough to follow and tickets printed in my home office. Between that and getting directions sent to my phone through cyberspace, I was all set to go.

My tour began at 2 p.m. and the day was rather mild for winter in Michigan, no real snowfall and a high temperature of about thirty-four degrees. I was just glad I wore an extra hoodie and brought my warmer gloves as the breeze was a little on the brisk side.

To my surprise, there was a light dusting of snow on the ground just north of Grand Rapids, so it did start to feel a little bit like Christmas.

Once checked in, I was invited to walk around the property. All of the in-season inhabitants were in their winter barn away from the public. However, their pens were well decorated for the holidays. All of the decorations were made by hand by various family members. Big, bright, and pleasant to the eye is a quick way to describe them.

I was very surprised how clean this area was. You could not tell that they had animals living in these pens for most of the year. If the cleanliness of the various pens and enclosures in any way reflect how they operate in season, then I will be sure to come back in the spring. And come back I did...during their opening week actually.

DAYS AND HOURS OF OPERATION

Deer Tracks Junction opens in April and offers the Hands-On experience through October. Then there is the holiday excursion that I described for you here.

MUST SEE

The Christmas Experience was rather neat. I would recommend it, even if the bulk of their inhabitants are on hiatus in their winter barn. Cindy Lou and Max checked me in. As we waited, the building started filling with other families joining us on this tour. At just about 2 p.m., the guests from the last tour started coming into the building to visit Santa and be on their way. Suddenly, the Grinch walked in and started greeting the children and harassing the adults from our party. The Grinch was also our tour guide/owner of the park.

We all loaded up into a large stagecoach-looking trailer pulled by a tractor. During the tour, we were educated by the Grinch all about the herbivores that he raises in the various paddocks throughout the property. We stopped at a number of stations where we were invited to feed a large variety of animals, including whitetail deer, elk, whitetail fawn, a couple of camel calves, and small herd of reindeer.

The Grinch kept us all entertained throughout the tour. I had a very enjoyable time.

Since many of the animals were kept in a barn over the winter, I decided to revisit Deer Tracks Junction in the spring. It was worth the drive over on Memorial Day to see the property come to life with a large number of animals as well as many children playing in and on the multitude of structures specifically designed for their enjoyment.

During the summer hours, you will have an opportunity to purchase feed for the various animals such as goats, pigs, camel, and even canaries. There were many potbelly piglets and helpers to let visitors pet them.

I walked into one small building where there were a pair of Nubian goats were being milked by the owner. One mother had given birth to triplets earlier in the week and needed help feeding her babies. The other mother had just given birth to an unusually large number of four kids and was not up to feeding them, either. Once milked, one of the staff bottle-fed each newborn to ensure they got the needed colostrum found only in the mother's milk. Colostrum had many vital nutrients that newborn mammals need to help in their survival.

FIELD NOTES

This park is part of a breeding program. They raise a large number of whitetail deer, elk, yaks, and other animals for sale. As I mentioned earlier, this is not a zoo. This is a working farm.

Keep an eye open for whitetail deer that have patches of white fur on their faces. Ask the staff what these particular deer are called. Also, ask if these unique creatures can get sunburned.

Spring is usually the time of year that most inhabitants here give birth. This might be a good time to schedule your hands-on experience. From what I have seen firsthand, hands-on is all summer long, regardless of animal age and size.

CONTACT INFORMATION

Deer Tracks Junction
7850 14 Mile Rd.
Cedar Springs, MI 49319
(616) 863-3337
Website: http://www.deertracksjunction.com/
info@deertracksjunction.com

❾ Detroit Zoo

TOWN

Royal Oak

DESCRIPTION AND EXPERIENCE

It has been quite a while since I had been to the Detroit Zoo. My last visit was part of my daughter's first birthday over twenty years ago. However, since this zoo is open year-round, I decided to do my research for this book during the harder months of winter.

The Detroit Zoo is open most days of the year. However, this winter they did close on the last day of January due to a crazy cold snap where surface temperatures read in the negative teens. This weather impacted the entire state for most of that week. Luckily, my visit was just a couple days later during a 70-degree warm-up.

Once I parked and pulled on my nice warm winter boots, I made my way to the gate with my prepaid tickets from their website. My first exhibit ended up being one of my favorites of the day.

It was the Polk Penguin Conservation Center. When I walked in, I was greeted by a large population of penguins in a mix of not one, but four species. These include the Gentoo, King, Macaroni, and Southern Rockhopper. They all appeared to be very active both in and out of the water.

There was a ramp walkway leading to the lower level of this exhibit. Luckily, there were handrails to hold onto, because the ramp became a surround-sound, live-motion video of a ship crashing through rough seas. Between that and the volume, it made for a rather interesting experience.

On the lower level, I learned about exploring the Antarctic. I am impressed with the level of toughness of these explorers to survive in such harsh conditions. Given the technology in clothing and equipment back in that time, I am sure not many of us would have made it.

At the bottom level, I got the opportunity to experience the penguins up close as they swam in a huge tank of water that simulates their natural habitat. I am simply amazed at their speed in the water versus their clumsy appearance on land.

With this being a winter visit, there were many inhabitants that were not out enjoying the snow. I had the chance to talk to a zookeeper about why the family of otters were not out, and it was due to all the ice over the water. It presented a potential hazard that they did not want to risk. However, as I passed the enclosure after this particular conversation, another zookeeper was using a spade to break the ice up. I am confident the Otter had a great time in the fresh snow.

This is a large zoo. You can easily plan to spend the entire day here, taking the time to enjoy everything. If you are a step counter, you will not be disappointed after your day here.

DAYS AND HOURS OF OPERATION

The Detroit Zoo is open year-round. Check their website to verify their hours of operations and other information.

MUST SEE

So, I highly recommend the Arctic Ring of Life exhibit that is toward the middle of the zoo. I had the opportunity to see a sleeping polar bear in a cave. She had a nice fresh bed of straw and was looking very comfortable. It was evident that the skulk arctic fox were enjoying the snow. All of the snow in their enclosure was trodden, and they were all napping in the sun. They provided a great photo opportunity.

Further on, I ran into a few grey and harbor seals that were bobbing in the water and then dropping out of sight. A few minutes after that, I was able to see them underwater as the path winds down to an entrance into a tunnel. The tunnel is impressive in that on one side, you can view the seals underwater, and on the other you can view the polar bear when they are swimming.

FIELD NOTES

As you are touring the exhibits, you will notice large buildings behind some of them. This is where the residents stay while their outdoor enclosures are being cleaned, or during the winter months when it is not safe for them to walk in the snow and ice.

Some animals such as the bears hibernate during the winter, so they are kept from being disturbed by us human onlookers.

Locate a zookeeper and ask which buildings are open to the public. It is a unique experience to see the inside accommodations provided to some of the animals here.

There are a number of buildings to tour that are well heated in the winter. These include the buildings that house the reptiles, amphibians, an aviary, and butterfly exhibits. The aviary was particularly relaxing for me. I could sit in there for hours if there was not so much to see.

CONTACT INFORMATION

Detroit Zoo
8450 W. Ten Mile Road
Royal Oak, MI 48067
(248) 541-5717
Website: https://www.detroitzoo.org/
Email through their "Contact Us" web page

ZOO AFFILIATIONS & SPONSORSHIPS

Association of Zoos & Aquariums (AZA)

⓾ DeYoung Family Zoo

TOWN

Wallace, Upper Peninsula

DESCRIPTION AND EXPERIENCE

This zoo is the furthest zoo from my doorstep. They are located so close to Wisconsin, that had I missed my turn, I might have found myself in the Badger State.

Bud DeYoung and Carrie Cramer opened their zoo to the public in 1990 and have been growing the park ever since. Their days between Memorial Day and Labor Day weekends offer a rather robust schedule of events to fill your entire day.

I planned my research visit during a long holiday weekend and included an overnight stay in Powers. I have never been to this part of the Upper Peninsula and it was a nice treat to do so finally. One item to note is that the zoo resides in the Central Standard

Time Zone, so if you rush from Escanaba at 9 a.m., you may find yourself waiting to park at about 9 a.m. CST.

I drove up just as they were opening the gates on a nice sunny morning. You can see some of the primates as you enter the parking lot. Once I paid my admission, I started my tour viewing the primates. There was a Japanese macaque peeking around a tree trunk at me. Every time I tried to snap a picture; she would promptly hide out of view.

If you come here to see many large animals, you will not be disappointed. They have three large enclosures that house different types of bears. There are also many tigers roaming in a few different enclosures as well, and let's not forget the camels.

A double layer of fencing surrounded all of these large enclosures. One unique thing I found about this structure type is that they intentionally grow various plants that serve as a food source for many of the inhabitants. Another thing that is very noticeable about many enclosures are the natural ponds inside them. There were bears enjoying the water, as well as a couple tigers. It did make for some nice zoom-in photography.

DAYS AND HOURS OF OPERATION

The DeYoung Family Zoo is open between April and October. These dates may change from year to year, as the weather in the high North can be unpredictable as to when winter really starts or ends.

MUST SEE

Posted throughout the zoo is a schedule of encounters that take visitors all around the park. You can easily tour the park on your own, as I did initially. However, I quickly found the various activities gave me a unique opportunity to learn more about some of the inhabitants, as well as a chance to feed a number of herbivores.

I did catch Mr. DeYoung discussing his Eurasian brown bears followed by tossing a number of watermelons up and over the fencing into the pond, where one of the bears clambered in and started eating one. I was able to zoom in with my camera for some interesting pictures.

During one presentation, Carrie gives an awesome story about the pack of timber wolves living there. She explains who they are, their current role in the pack, and how they got there. This interesting story ends with a song.

FIELD NOTES

Visit the Education Pavilion often. Various staff members will bring out any number of animals during their encounter activity. I was able to hold a bearded dragon, hold a rescued red kangaroo joey, and touch the fur of an arctic fox kit.

Sometimes nature can be cruel. We all got to meet a four-day old whitetail deer fawn they were bottle feeding because its mother and twin were lost during birth. Bud explained to us what has to be done to try to mimic the mother's care to help this infant survive. This little doe will most likely be introduced into the herd of whitetail deer once she is older and eating on her own.

CONTACT INFORMATION

DeYoung Family Zoo
N5406 County Road 577
Wallace, MI 49893
(906) 788-4093
Website: http://thedeyoungfamilyzoo.com
zooquestions@yahoo.com

Zoo Tip:

Zoos are a
great place
to
people watch.

⑪ GarLyn Zoo

TOWN:

Naubinway, Upper Peninsula

DESCRIPTION AND EXPERIENCE

I have seen this zoo advertised by brochure for a number of years. It so happened that a few of us were running a bridge race that is famous each fall in Mackinaw City. After that fun, yet tiring, experience, we wanted to take on some more adventure. So, we decided to venture north by traveling west on Hwy 2 out of St. Ignace.

The GarLyn Zoo sets on a 30-acre piece of land just about 40 minutes from the north end of the Mackinaw Bridge. Lynn and Gary Moore started the zoo in 1994, and it continues to grow a little bit each year. This zoo is one of many family-owned establishments in Michigan, showing us that caring for animals is a passion that grows with the family as the family grows.

It was mid-afternoon and a tad warm outside, which was odd for an early September afternoon. Most of the inhabitants were not overly active, as they were trying to stay cool. I thought it might have been nap time…but only for a moment.

That was when we noticed something very unique and amazing. Zoo staff members started walking to the various enclosures, talking to the animals. The animals quickly started responding by actively interacting with these folks. Granted, it was probably due to these park employees being their primary caregivers, but who cares...the animals became active!

Most memorable was when another staff member walked towards us from the back of an enclosure. She was walking on the outside of the fenced area that housed a cougar. At first, we did not see this magnificent creature, but then we noticed it stalking this young woman. All of a sudden, she started running towards us. The odd thing was that she had a smile on her face. Then, we saw the cougar shoot out in a full run, chasing her. For the unsuspecting, we definitely got a start, as we did not know what was going on.

After this unusual and breathtaking interaction, we approached this young woman to see if she was okay and what we just witnessed. She was all too happy to explain that they play this game every day to help maintain some of the cougar's wild habits and promote a little human-to-animal physical fitness.

While revisiting over Memorial Day weekend, I learned an important thing. Zoos seem to keep changing. There were more enclosures this second time. This is due in part to increasing numbers of species that live here. In addition, there is the growing needs of other inhabitants as they, or their family gets larger.

Speaking of growing families, I spent an easy half hour watching the baby ring-tailed lemur jumping and climbing all over the enclosure. There were also the couple of young sika deer, one of which was only a week old. I also noticed a caribou calf nursing from its mother.

Many of the animals in the park have been raised or handled by humans most of their lives. This helps ensure that animals and caregivers maintain a healthy and safe relationship while working together. The staff interaction with the animals does promote a caring atmosphere.

DAYS AND HOURS OF OPERATION

The GarLyn Zoo is open from May 1st through the end of October. Opening time is at 10 a.m. each day.

MUST SEE

In the bear enclosure, see if you can find a domesticated roommate. Learn the story of how this animal and bear came to be friends. Asking a staff member questions about them can also provide entertaining and educational answers.

The large cats are interesting to watch as they were enjoying their recently constructed wooden platforms. This structure significantly improved viewing and picture taking. They are now closer to eye level. I was able to get a couple of decent shots with my camera.

FIELD NOTES

I have never seen so many chickens and guinea fowl in any one place before; however, there are multitudes of them here. They are all free-ranging, including a plethora of colorful and albino peacocks. There were many nice photo opportunities with this collection of birds, and many of them turned out rather nicely.

There is no need to apply bug spray to your children, as the park prides itself in maintaining a natural insect repellant around the park. Smart thinking, as they do not want the animals getting sick due to the toxins from such sprays. What is this repellant you ask? Well, as you are walking down all the pathways in the park you will notice that you are stepping on a nice cushion of cedar mulch. This cedar mulch deters the insects. I did not have any issues with bugs inside the property, but that did change once back out in the parking lot...true story.

CONTACT INFORMATION

Contact Information
GarLyn Zoological Park, Inc.
P.O.Box 245 / W9104 US2
Naubinway, Michigan 49762-0245
(906) 477-1085
Website: www.garlunzoo.com
info@garlynzoo.com

⑫ GT Butterfly House & Bug Zoo

TOWN

Williamsburg

DESCRIPTION AND EXPERIENCE

Okay, so you may be asking yourself, a butterfly house with bugs as a zoo? Seriously? The cool thing I found about writing this book is that I can write about anything I want. However, this establishment is no different from other parks covered in this book. They offer a unique chance to experience a large number of brightly colored creatures up close and personal.

Initial research shows there are only two butterfly houses in Michigan. The one I included in this book, and the other on Mackinac Island. The one here in Williamsburg is a fairly new zoo opening up to the public in 2014, just two short years after Cyndie Roach began setting her vision for making it happen.

I had the opportunity to recruit a couple of assistants on this particular trip with my daughter and grandson who live not too far away in Houghton Lake. As we walked into the entrance, a large group of kindergartners from a local school followed us. As we paid for admission, we were invited to look about on our own, or we could join one of the two groups they had formed with the school children, teachers, and chaperones. We chose to join the group going into the butterfly house.

With the skylights, the room was very well lit. There were a number of butterflies fluttering around or resting on various plants and feeders. A number of them were found on flowers drinking nectar. There were several flowering plants all around, making the entire room dance with color.

The bugkeepers are all very knowledgeable about all the insects and other creatures living there. They even have a special baby butterfly release with each group of guests for some interactive fun. Near one entrance to the butterfly house there is an observation window where you may be able to watch butterflies hatch from their chrysalises. You may also see any number of newly hatched butterflies and moths.

It can take from an hour to a solid hour-and-a-half to enjoy all the creatures here. They host many school field trips and it is definitely worth the drive to visit. My grandson was only eighteen months old and enjoyed looking at everything and watching the butterflies flutter around him.

DAYS AND HOURS OF OPERATION

The GT Butterfly House & Bug Zoo opens in May and runs through early October. Check out their website, as the park hours may change around some of the holidays.

MUST SEE

Everything here at the butterfly house is a must see. However, you might easily overlook some of the Bug Zoo. They have a working honeybee hive where you can see the bees working away. They have quite an impressive collection of tarantulas and other large insects.

Near the end of the Bug Zoo live a number of creatures that are not even bugs; however, they are very unusual and interesting to look at. There is some informational signage, but the best facts to learn about these animals will come from the bugkeepers themselves.

FIELD NOTES

What do you do when a butterfly lands on your butt? Well, after getting a number of giggles and snickers from the school children, teachers, chaperones, and yes, even my daughter, I slowly walked over to one of the kind bugkeepers for assistance. They have a special butterfly-handling tool for just such situations when a butterfly wants to hang out with you...literally. They use a small paintbrush to safely shoo the insect off the human's person...or "bum" in my case.

While we toured the GT Butterfly House and Bug Zoo, one of the handlers brought out a very unusual insect. It was long and brown, and kind of looks like a stick. It was not the "Common Walking Stick" insect of North America, but was the Giant Spiny Stick insect (Eurycantha calcarata) from New Guinea, which is much larger. The bug keeper told us all about this insect and then let us carefully touch its back. It actually felt like a stick.

Ask about the creature called the Axolotl that can regenerate parts of its body. The staff here are very excited to tell you all about this amazing creature and how regeneration works. They also have an interesting story to tell about their Iberian ribbed newt named Squishy that uses its ribcage to perform a couple of different life-preservation feats.

CONTACT INFORMATION

GT Butterfly House & Bug Zoo
8840 M 72 E
Williamsburg, MI 49690
(231) 944-0774
Website: http://www.gtbutterflyzoo.com/
info@gtbutterflyzoo.com

Zoo Tip:

See everything twice. Animals move around.

⓭ Howell Nature Center

TOWN

Howell

DESCRIPTION AND EXPERIENCE

Since this center is open year-round, I decided to experience it in the winter months. Doing a little research, I discovered they were offering a seminar on how to photograph birds of prey. Since I am an amateur photographer, I signed up for this session, as well as a guided tour of the property before the seminar.

The Howell Nature Center takes in several thousand animals a year. Many come in injured, are rehabilitated, and then released back into the wild. Some cannot be released due to their injuries being too severe. Examples include amputation, partial amputation, and in many cases, blindness or other physical impairment.

So, what do you do with these injured creatures? Well, you use them for educational purposes, and the center does a great job of it as they host several field trips all through the school year.

I do not discuss pricing in this book, but this property offers a very reasonable admission price. The property also offers a large play area for children of all ages. In the summer, it includes a waterfall and stream in which to cool down.

A group of us met at 10 a.m. on a Sunday morning to tour the property. Being winter, there was some snow on the grounds and a little ice here and there. **Tip for Success**: Dressing appropriately is key to any weather conditions year-round. Warmer boots on my part would have been helpful.

Our first stop was to visit a coyote. I have a number of farming friends that find these guys a nuisance, but this one was very healthy, active, and just fun to watch. It was explained to us that this coyote cannot be returned to the wild due to lack of hunting skills, since it was raised as a pet originally.

Our tour group also got a great look at a red fox. These animals all looked very large, but that was due to their winter coats. In the spring, as the temperatures start to climb, they will molt, or shed, this extra bit of fur.

The property is well laid out and includes an enclosure that houses a couple of whitetail deer doe. One of them was accidently adopted by a dog that found it as a fawn in the wild. Somehow, this dog coaxed the fawn out of hiding and to follow him home to his master.

DAYS AND HOURS OF OPERATION

The Howell Nature Center is open year-round. Check their website for hours and upcoming events.

MUST SEE

There are many birds of prey here. Our guide did a great job describing each type and how each bird came to be here. Many have vision or flight issues, so they cannot hunt on their own. Many of these birds are trained and used for educational purposes.

The bobcat was perched up high, giving us all a nice viewing and photo-op as well. To share a tip for photographic success...if an animal is not cooperating with your picture taking efforts, come back to the enclosure later. There is always a decent chance that the subject will get up and move. Give yourself more opportunities to catch them doing so.

There is a male turkey in one enclosure, and we were told that the ladies that live in the area like to stop by to visit him. So, apparently his strutting around his pen is working on attracting potential mates. Unfortunately, he is not allowed outside his enclosure to romance the ladies.

FIELD NOTES

So, the photography seminar was an unexpected add-on to my research of the Howell Nature Center. The seminar included a fantastic presentation and slideshow from an award-winning photographer that travels the world with other photographers to shoot many types of birds and other animals in the wild.

After the presentation and a nice lunch, we were invited to drive to another section of the property. When we got there and parked, we were allowed to shoot many different birds of prey. Each bird had at least one handler and we were invited and encouraged to get as close as we wanted to get some decent shots.

Our group spent a good two hours in the frigid winter afternoon walking back and forth shooting a screech owl, an American kestrel snowy owl, barn owl, redtail hawk, horned owl, and an American bald eagle, taking thousands of pictures from a number of different vantage points.

Camera types there ranged from extremely large lenses and heavy tripods to department store cameras like mine, to a cell phone. Of the 550 pictures I took, I believe that about two of each bird turned out. Regardless, it was a great time!

A final note about the Howell Nature Center: ask the staff about their "imprinted" birds, and what that means. You should find it interesting.

CONTACT INFORMATION

Howell Nature Center
1005 Triangle Lake Road
Howell, MI 48843
(517) 546-0249
Website: http://www.howellnaturecenter.org/
hcnc@howellnaturecenter.org

⑭ Indian Creek Zoo

TOWN

Lambertville. It is about six miles east of Hwy 223 just north of the Michigan-Ohio state line.

DESCRIPTION AND EXPERIENCE

This is one of the newest zoos in Michigan, open to the public since 2014 after Joe Garverick responded to a growing number of requests from area schools wanting to tour his property. He applied to the Department of Agriculture and became licensed to open his zoo to the public.

The day I toured, the local meteorologist called for a warm and muggy day; however, I lucked into overcast skies for the duration of my visit. When I paid to get into the park, there were options to purchase a large cup full of sliced carrots to feed the animals. The cashier let me know that animals allowed to receive these treats would have a large smiley face posted on signs outside the enclosures. That is a smart idea and made it rather easy for visitors of all ages to understand who could and could not be fed.

There are a number of exhibits here and plenty of room for growth. Walking into the park, I was greeted by a majestic looking timber wolf. Near the wolf was a large enclosure where I could walk amongst and feed an impressive colony of rabbits.

There is an nice primate section with large enclosures. Each inhabitant had plenty of room to play. Many of the exhibits around the park supplied ample room for its occupants. I was most impressed with the space allotted to the North American bobcat. It was hard to spot them at first, but once found, made for some great viewing.

There was evidence of successful animal breeding, as I could see a jocy moving around inside its mother's pouch. Other evidence of successful breeding was found in a couple of very spacious sections that house whitetail deer. Each of the two enclosures housed a doe and twin fawns. These awesome creatures are used to being fed, and one fawn was happy to let me pet it while the mom was busy eating the offering of carrots.

There appears to be a lot of property that is not yet developed. I am curious to see what future additions might bring.

DAYS AND HOURS OF OPERATION

The Indian Creek Zoo is open between April and December.

MUST SEE

There are three ostriches that are popular in the park. They are even iconized in a painting on the property wall. You can also get close enough to this trio to feed them. They were close enough to me, but I was a little wary of them. Please do not judge me...these are some pretty big birds to be up-close to. I found them to be awe-inspiring yet intimidating.

Look out for the various petting stations scattered through the park. While there, I got to pet baby rabbits called kits, young goats called kids, and a family of hedgehogs called hoglets.

FIELD NOTES

Ration your supply of carrot sticks so you can feed the giraffe named Sudoku. Try holding the carrot stick with one hand and touch the snout for a cool experience. He was very docile to the guests offering him a treat.

Take some awesome pictures of parrots that are not living behind enclosures, bars, or netting.

The American bald eagles and owls are always impressive to watch. If you see a zookeeper nearby, ask them what each bird of prey prefers to eat there.

See how many camels you can find. You might be able to ride one as well.

CONTACT INFORMATION

Indian Creek Zoo
2740 Consear Road
Lambertville, MI 48144
(734) 224-0390
Website: http://www.indiancreekzoo.com
indiancreekzoo@aol.com

Zoo Tip:

Zoos are a great place to people watch.

⓯ John Ball Zoo Society

TOWN

Downtown, Grand Rapids

DESCRIPTION AND EXPERIENCE

I have driven through Grand Rapids a number of times and usually enjoy (NOT) being caught up in "big city driving" as I call it. In running an errand just north of the city, we looked up the John Ball Zoo on my GPS to find that it was only about an eleven-minute drive away. The mapping application also plotted a course that had me take less traveled streets instead of getting on the highway.

Upon walking up a hill from the gates to the park epicenter, I was greeted by a beautiful pair of bald eagles. Nice way to start the tour...with a little patriotism.

So, the one best piece of advice I can give about this park is to make sure you are wearing comfortable shoes. The park has a nice layout, and some paths and walkways that wind around and up and down the property. The entire property is hillier than the parking lot might lead you to believe. Actually, I enjoyed walking the property but will be sure to keep sensible shoes stowed in my vehicle for next time.

I did take the opportunity to speak with a young woman that was cleaning out the flamingo pen. She was in the zoo's internship program while working on her master's degree in zoology. I asked her what areas of the park she liked working in the best. She replied that the chimpanzees and some of the mammals housed in the reptile building were her favorite.

Overall, the park was well staffed, and they had food and beverage stations all over the park. My running joke was, "You could not throw a snow cone without hitting a different snow cone station." On a hot day, that could be a good thing.

DAYS AND HOURS OF OPERATION

The John Ball Zoo is open to the public between Spring through mid-Fall. They keep an updated calendar of their days and hours on their website.

MUST SEE

I was most impressed with the tiger enclosure. When I first saw these magnificent beasts, they were behind a very large glass wall. I could easily view them as they walked around or chose to nap. As I was moving on to find the next exhibits, I observed a tunnel of heavy fencing up high at the edge of the park. I was not sure what that was all about until I walked up to another tiger enclosure that sported a nice pool. It was then I realized that the tigers could roam back and forth between enclosures. As an observation, I bet a motivated tiger could gain a lot of speed running through the tunnel.

The Wild Way Trail is also an interesting area of the park. The entrance includes two sets of large gates. Once inside, two zookeepers and a court of kangaroo greeted me. The kangaroo were all resting outside of the path, but I was informed that they usually move freely amongst us humans. These two zookeepers were also full of information about the creatures under their charge.

Further down was an interesting exhibit of Lemur. Their habitat included an over-ground tunnel that expanded across the trail I was walking down. It allowed for an open viewing experience, and I think I watched and snapped pictures for about twenty minutes.

FIELD NOTES

To see an array of animals, visit the reptile house. It is home to a number of reptiles and mammals. The glass viewing panes were clean, and I figured out how to reduce the glare while taking pictures. I would use my one hand to block light at the spot I was pointing my camera.

Talking to one of the zookeepers, I learned that many of the large cats like tigers, lions, and mountain lion for example are on exhibit only and there are no breeding programs allowed in Michigan due to state law. However, it was nice to hear they have had success with some of the primates.

Tip for an educational success...talk to the zookeepers that have a moment to chat. As I was leaving the park, there was another zookeeper exiting the bald eagle enclosure. She had just fed them. Upon asking what they eat, she stated, "Sometimes they get quail, sometimes they get fish, and sometimes they get chicken." I then asked what their favorite food is, and I found out it currently is the fish.

CONTACT INFORMATION

John Ball Zoo Society
1300 West Fulton Street
Grand Rapids, MI 49504
(616) 336-4301
Website: http://www.johnballzoosociety.org/
info@jbzoo.org

ZOO AFFILIATIONS & SPONSORSHIPS

Association of Zoos & Aquariums (AZA)

Zoo Tip:

Have a question?
Ask a Zookeeper.
They know a lot,
and love to share.

⑯ Lewis Farms & Petting Zoo

TOWN

New Era

DESCRIPTION AND EXPERIENCE

Lewis Farms & Petting Zoo are just about a half mile off US31. I think a quarter of a mile of that distance is a parking lot for what I believe is a nice little tourism gem. I showed up at about 9:45 a.m. on a Sunday and found the parking lot in front of their market store already full of guests waiting for the doors to open.

Promptly at 10 a.m., a set of barn-type doors slid open to the right and left, and we were greeted and welcomed inside, where we wound around to one of many open registers. When paying admission, the clerk offered a souvenir cup filled with treats to feed the inhabitants. I thought the admission price, with the food, to be an exceptional deal.

Quick tip for success: If you wish to interact with some of the animals and perhaps get a great photo or two, buying food there is the best way to go. The animals are all very docile and will eagerly walk up to the guests in hopes of getting a treat or two.

The staff was very friendly, and I even got to chat with the owner, Cindy Lewis, for a minute. She was busy waiting on customers that were there for the bakery foods and hot coffee. She was nice enough to give me a few minutes to discuss the petting zoo portion of their operation.

DAYS AND HOURS OF OPERATION

Lewis Farms & Petting Zoo is open to the public near Mother's Day and operates daily until about the end of August. They open at 9 a.m. most days, reserving Sunday for the animals to sleep in an hour until 10 a.m.

MUST SEE

One thing I noticed right away when I entered the petting zoo area is that all these animals know what a souvenir cup is. From the goats, to the llamas, to the donkeys, and ponies, they all like to be fed treats. The goats and deer get excited for treats.

Tip for Success...in feeding larger groups of animals such as the goats or deer, the larger animals tend to push the smaller ones out of the way. In order to feed the smaller ones, I found it easy to do by placing treats in both hands. One hand goes to the larger, pushier of the bunch, and the other hand goes to the smaller animal that I wanted to feed in the first place.

Their dromedary camels also like these treats, and they were very careful about taking the food from my open hand. They can be intimidating, being such large creatures, but I quickly learned that holding the treats lower to the ground helped. They are talented at taking the food with their lips and are extremely gentle.

The miniature zebu were a very docile breed of small cows. They are not shy about coming up to take the treats from your hand. It was interesting that one of them had a soft and dry snout, while the other one was a little wetter and slobberier. Not that I minded it...just an observation.

You cannot go wrong entering the aviary that houses hundreds of colorful parakeets. You can buy sticks with seeds on them so they will land on your hand, arm, and shoulders to get their turn at eating them. At first, I did not buy any seed sticks but then talked myself into it. Since my souvenir cup was empty by that point, I asked the attendant to place the stick into the cup so I could have a chance to get my camera phone ready to take pictures. Smart call on my part, since as soon as I lifted the seed stick, I was lighted on by one parakeet, then three, then upwards to seven. It was a neat experience.

You could easily fill over half a day here at the petting zoo. However, if you want to fill your day, you could plan your day to include a drive to the Little Sable Lighthouse, which is only about twenty-five minutes away. With the nearby sand dunes, if the petting zoo does not tire you out, then walking the dunes might.

FIELD NOTES

Will an emu eat these treats that the other mammals were eating? I found out by placing a few nuggets in my open hand and found out that, yes, they like them very much. I was amazed how precise the emu was in snatching up one nugget at a time with its massive beak.

Among the inhabitants here on the farm is a national celebrity. Jeffrey the Camel was recorded walking into a local Pets Smart store that prides itself in welcoming pets inside. Talking with owner, Cindy Lewis, she told me that they were training Jeffrey to load himself into a trailer to be hauled from place to place for public appearances. He did a perfect job on the first try, so Cindy suggested on the second day they take Jeffrey to this large pet supply store. They did call ahead and went inside right at opening time to not cause too big a stir. However, with social media as it is, in less than forty-eight hours Jeffrey was being mentioned and shown on some local and national news outlets.

When you look at the court of wallabies, take a close look at their pouches. I did just that and noticed a joey head sticking out. The mother was very docile and let me get very close to her to take a photo.

Lewis Farm & Petting Zoo is so much more than a bakery and petting zoo. There are so many activities children can participate in around the park. Most of it is included with the price of admission. They have a homemade Skee-Ball game in the back of an old truck and throwing games with basketballs, footballs, and baseballs as well. They even have an entire building where children can play in an arena filled with shelled corn.

CONTACT INFORMATION

Lewis Farms & Petting Zoo
4180 West M-20
New Era, Michigan 49446
(231) 861-5730
Website: https://visitlewisfarms.com/
media@visitlewisfarms.com

⑰ Oswald's Bear Ranch

TOWN

Newberry, Upper Peninsula

DESCRIPTION AND EXPERIENCE

This unique establishment opened to the public in 1997 and is a bear-only ranch that is home to a large number of rescued and abandoned bears. Being from the Lower Peninsula, I made it an extended weekend to tour our UP zoos and other unique wildlife establishments.

Dean Oswald started rescuing orphaned cubs and is pretty much the backstory for the park as it is today. He plays a very active role in running the ranch with his family. It all seemed very organized, and there were many people there already enjoying some personal time with all these bears.

The rain had washed through the area the night before my visit. And, the morning fog did not want to dissipate during most of my drive up. However, when I got there, the mist seemed to stop completely, and I was able to pull out my good camera to use.

There are several rather large enclosures on the property. The males, females, and juvenile bears live in separate areas from each other. Each space has a double fence to help keep the bears safe from us humans. Or, is that the other way around? Oh well. Each enclosure also has an observation deck where you can get an unhampered view and photographs of the bears.

If you are looking to add other tourism options to your day, you can add the GarLyn Zoo as part of a zoomarathon. Alternatively, the Tahquamenon Falls State Park is just about a half-hour drive from the ranch. There is also the Logging Museum not far from Oswald's on M-123. Either way, it is easy to make a full day in this portion of the Upper Peninsula.

DAYS AND HOURS OF OPERATION

Oswald's Bear Ranch is open from the Friday of Memorial Day weekend through the end of September. Check their website or travel brochure for hours of operation.

MUST SEE

For a smaller park, I was surprised how large and busy their gift shop was. I do not normally write about gift shops, but in this one, there were many unique items pertaining to bears.

The bear cubs are always a treat to watch. When they are not posing for pictures with humans, they like to roughhouse with each other in their pen. They exhibited high levels of energy on this particular day. For an extra fee, you can have pictures taken with the cubs. I did not partake this time but will add that to my bucket list of things to do next time.

If bears hibernate through the winter, where do they sleep? When walking the many paths surrounding each enclosure, take care to look around into the wooded areas. I was able to spot a couple of dens in the one female enclosure. This particular enclosure is over a half-mile around.

FIELD NOTES

I had the opportunity to speak with Mr. Oswald while I was there and asked if he ever had issues with roaming bulls (male bear) trying to get into the female enclosures. He responded by telling me that there are no longer wild bear in the area. However, he did voice his concern over the wolf population.

Feel free to ask any of the family members questions about their inhabitants. If they cannot answer it, they have no qualms about pointing you to the man who can give you the best answer.

Feeding the bears? For a nominal fee, you can purchase a bag of apple slices. I did not see one single bear turn down an apple. While walking around the female perimeter fencing, there was a bear not 20 feet from me. The only way to give her an apple slice was to toss it up and over two very tall fences. I was careful to toss it high and short so the apple slice landed near her so she would not have to wander far to get it.

At the time of this writing, the Oswald family had just begun developing another mile of property for additional enclosures. When I asked Mr. Oswald what they were going to put there, and he simply stated that he has not yet decided.

CONTACT INFORMATION

Oswald's Bear Ranch
13814 County Road 407
Newberry, MI 49868
(906) 293-3147
Website: http://www.oswaldsbearranch.com/

ZOO AFFILIATIONS & SPONSORSHIPS

Zoological Association of America (ZAA)

Zoo Tip:
Zoos attract children.
Let your inner child
have a
little fun as well.

⑱ Potter Park Zoo

TOWN

Lansing

DESCRIPTION AND EXPERIENCE

I have decided that if I lived or worked close enough to a zoo, I would invest in an annual pass. I find zoos as relaxing places to walk through, animal watch, people watch, and just have a relaxing time. Potter Park Zoo would be a good candidate for me.

Potter Park was dedicated on July 5, 1915 and added twenty-seven acres more land in 1917. With Potter Park Zoo's official opening in 1920, it became Michigan's first public zoo. The next year a pavilion was completed, one of the zoo's first buildings.

The day was sunny and a little on the warm side when I came to tour. I walked through the gates in the early afternoon on a weekday, and it was not too busy. It had been several years since I had visited this park, and I noticed a number of new enclosures.

Probably one of the most impressive enclosures was the one that housed their red pandas. It was very spacious and filled with many items for them to climb on while offering decent viewing for us humans. When I walked by the exhibit the first time, I observed a single red panda inside a smaller indoor chamber which had a large glass pane to look through. A couple of hours later, I walked past the enclosure again to find at least two red pandas walking and climbing around in the outside area.

DAYS AND HOURS OF OPERATION

Potter Park Zoo is open year-round. Their hours change throughout the year, so checking beforehand on their website might save you some time.

MUST SEE

Once you are in the park, there should be a listing of activities going on at various locations around the zoo. If you do not find the listing, the park office is near the entrance where you can ask for the schedule. I highly suggest asking at the park entrance where you can locate a list of times and locations where zookeepers share their expertise with the public on different animals located there.

Different zoos call these activities by different names such as Animal Encounter, Meet the Zookeeper, and Excursion for example.

When the otters are active, they are a hoot to watch. They have a lot of energy and are very inquisitive. Surprisingly, I was able to catch one of them standing still long enough to snap a good picture or two. As hard as they play, they often nap just as hard. If you catch them in a nap, make it a point to revisit them later. All I can say is that it is a tough life being an otter.

The lion exhibit was impressive. There is one section that is a large glass-viewing pane. It is amazing how large these cats are as they were stretched out and dozing on a pile of huge boulders. I was able to get a few nice pictures of the pads on paws. Their paws are huge!

FIELD NOTES

I had a great talk with one of the zookeepers at the tiger exhibit. She stated that they keep their two tigers separated by having them take turns between the indoor and outdoor enclosures. The zoo has a series of tunnels underground that help keep the tigers from interacting during this shift change.

When I asked her about their breeding program, she stated that overall, the numbers of births vary from year to year. There was a successful birthing in the otter enclosure, as the female had a pair of male pups. They were more like juveniles when I saw them, but I did witness a strong bond between them and their mother.

CONTACT INFORMATION

Potter Park Zoo
1301 S. Pennsylvania Avenue
Lansing, MI 48912
(517) 483-4222
Website: http://www.potterparkzoo.org
zoocontact@ingham.org

ZOO AFFILIATIONS & SPONSORSHIPS

Association of Zoos & Aquariums (AZA)

⑲ Roscommon Zoo

TOWN

Roscommon

DESCRIPTION AND EXPERIENCE

The Roscommon Zoo is a perfect place to stop and stretch your legs for an hour or two during your journeys up north or down state. They are only about thirteen minutes away from Interstate-75 and twenty-five minutes from Michigan Hwy-127.

This property used to be called Cindy Lou's Petting Zoo and was open to the public for about thirteen years. The owners were looking at relocating the animals as part of their closing the property due to declining structural conditions. It was then that Rachelle and Andrew Gehringer stepped up to take over the operation. They quickly began reconstruction and new construction to help ensure the health and safety of their inhabitants. Around 2015, they reopened the property as the Roscommon Zoo.

My visit came on a rainy Sunday afternoon in May. Though the forecast threatened thunderstorms all day, it was not even sprinkling when I drove into the parking lot just before noon. Even with spending time talking with this family of three, I had a solid two hours to enjoy the zoo and highly active animals before the rain really started to come down. **Tip for Success**…prepare yourself for inclement weather. It never hurts to stow a rain jacket and boots so a little thing like rain or standing water does not ruin your tour.

I took advantage with my admission to include a bag of carrot sticks and a bag of kangaroo and monkey treats. My first animal encounter included two lively donkeys. They enjoyed the carrots, and shortly after beginning my tour, I realized that I should have invested in the bucket of carrots instead of the smaller bag.

The ponies and llamas were also very gentle in taking carrots from my hand. There is signage throughout the park placed near the animals that should not be offered treats. The reason some animals cannot enjoy these treats is due to their own special dietary needs.

If you want a good giggle, take a look at the angora sheep that are in the enclosure with the goats. One of them looked more like a cartoon character than a real animal. They are a hoot, and they all wanted more treats than I had to offer.

DAYS AND HOURS OF OPERATION

The Roscommon Zoo is open to the public during most weekends in May and then open daily beginning mid-June through October. If there is a forecast of possible inclement or severe weather, I suggest calling them or checking their Facebook page about their hours that day.

MUST SEE

There are over 120 animals sorted into various types and sizes of pens and enclosures. The inside of the park is actually visible from the road, where you may see a number of geese and their black swan.

The Gehringer family have been busy making improvements to the park, and they keep adding more exhibits. One structure that stands out as the best in the state, is their peacock enclosure. There is plenty of room for the two peahens and two peacocks. This is especially important, as the males fan open their mass of tail feathers to impress the ladies. This enclosure allows for better picture taking because of the type of fencing used.

Their court of kangaroo are friendly and some of them will come up to you to receive one of the treats that can be purchased with admission. At my first encounter I offered one of the females a small caramel rice cake. She took it from me and then dropped it onto the ground. That was when the youngest family member and zookeeper said to me "Yeah, she likes the cheesy corn puffs better." So, I dug into my treat bag and pulled out a cheesy corn puff, and yep, she really enjoyed it. Luckily, this doe was not wasteful and did eat my original offering.

The tigers were fun to watch. Though it was overcast and cool when I went, they have large tanks for bathing in during those warmer summer days. When I first walked towards their enclosure, their younger tiger was in her stalking mode, watching me from behind a platform. I found out later that she was raised from a cub, and this was part of her play routine.

I always enjoy watching the large cats, and there are more than just tigers at Roscommon Zoo. Be sure to check out the other feline inhabitants. Some of the newly created enclosures will be housing some of them.

FIELD NOTES

When you visit the troop of kangaroo, look at their pouches and see if you can see any movement. When I was there, a couple of them had joeys, but they were still too young to begin peeking outside. Besides, it was a cooler spring day when I went. What marsupial would willingly want to leave all that warmth and comfort on a chilly day? I wouldn't.

During each day, the zookeepers will offer an up-close and personal look at a number of creatures there. I had the honor of feeling the body shell of a southern three-banded armadillo. This one originates from central and eastern Bolivia, the Mato Grasso of central Brazil, Chaco region of Paraguay, northern and central Argentina. Their shell feels rubbery, much like that of the alligator. Hard to compare if you have never held an alligator before. I actually had that experience at Critchlow's Alligator Sanctuary in Union City.

This family of zookeepers is very knowledgeable about all the creatures in their care. Ask them which ones are rescue animals. Another question could include asking about which animals may have been born or raised there.

Be sure to visit the potbelly pigs. The smaller one was up at the fence and did not care that I was out of treats by the time I got to her. She was just as happy to have her nose scratched and behind her ears.

CONTACT INFORMATION

Roscommon Zoo
6327 N. Michigan Hwy 18
Roscommon, MI 48653
(989) 275-4500
Website: http://www.roscommonzoo.com/

⑳ Sea Life Michigan Aquarium

TOWN

Auburn Hills

DESCRIPTION AND EXPERIENCE

Since this is a year-round indoor facility. It ended up being a very mild day early in February, just after a couple of extremely frigid days. Sea Life is only about a half hour drive north of the Detroit Zoo, so it made sense to include it in my zoo marathon plans.

Sea Life resides inside the Great Lakes Crossing Outlets just off Interstate 75. You could easily make a day trip right here as long as you enjoy getting in a great variety of shopping. There are over 185 attractions, stores, and restaurants there.

Once checked into the aquarium, I joined a line of people waiting to enter the main doors into the aquarium. It was easy to tell that this aquarium experience is designed for children, because there were sea creature cartoon characters representing Sea Life Aquarium. Just before the main entry was a gentleman having fun with guests by taking their pictures in multiple poses in front of a green screen. After photos are taken, guests move to a holding area to wait their turn to enter a doorway into the aquarium. They let about thirty people in at a time to help keep the aquarium from becoming overcrowded.

When I entered this main door, the group I was with entered another holding area. After the doors behind us closed, a small video started playing where the digitized hosts greeted us. They explained "conservation" and took us into the sea. Shortly after, another set of doors open up to a path that leads us through the aquarium.

The exhibits are well laid out, and it was not overly congested with humans. This is due in part to the timing of new groups being admitted into this area. Smart idea! I was very impressed how by clean and clear the tanks were. I took a number of photos with my cell phone camera, and a large number of them turned out.

DAYS AND HOURS OF OPERATION

The Sea Life Michigan Aquarium is open year-round. For a better experience entering the facility, they recommend purchasing tickets in advance online.

MUST SEE

The aquarium can be walked through in about an hour; however, my ticket allowed unlimited access for the day. Fish-gaze, shop, get lunch at any number or restaurants there in the outlet mall, then fish-gaze some more.

If you have children along on this adventure, it will take more than an hour to tour the aquarium. Located in the aquarium are a couple interactive stations. One includes a hands-on experience where you can touch some creatures in a shallow pool. There are keepers there to help ensure the safety of these creatures and humans alike. They are very knowledgeable about the creatures in these shallow pools. I encourage you to ask questions.

There are activity stations available where everyone (including adults) can color a page that has a number of different fishes on it.

FIELD NOTES

While touring the aquarium, take the time to gaze into the various tanks; you will find more than just fish. There were a number of plant life that are equally important for sea life to thrive, not to mention that many tanks offer several different types of fish to look at.

Not sure what a brightly colored fish is called? Not a problem here, as there are video displays all over that describe each resident in each tank.

Check out the digital fish tanks. This is where you have a chance to create and color your own fish. After a few moments, you can view your fish as it swims in the fish tank. You can even take your fish home, thanks to some digital magic. Just note you will need a QR Code reader on your smartphone.

CONTACT INFORMATION

Sea Life Michigan Aquarium
Great Lakes Crossing Outlets, 4316 Baldwin
Road
Auburn Hills, MI 48326
(866) 622-0605
Website:
https://www.visitsealife.com/Michigan
sealifeMichigan@sealifeus.com

ZOO AFFILIATIONS & SPONSORSHIPS

Association of Zoos & Aquariums (AZA)

Zoo Tip:

Pack extra batteries, USB chargers, and memory cards.

㉑ The Creature Conservancy

TOWN

Ann Arbor

DESCRIPTION AND EXPERIENCE

I live just about an hour away from Ann Arbor, and for all the times I have been there, I never knew this place existed. So, a little research can uncover all sorts of hidden gems in our great state of Michigan. The Creature Conservancy is no exception!

From their website, I was able to inquire about reservations for a private tour. The tour has a base fee that covers entry for two guests. The total party size can be up to five people. A couple of days later, I received a phone call to discuss the tour and finalize the reservation. We discussed some of the rules and expectations, and then finalized the number of people on this tour.

I decided to schedule this tour during the winter since they are open year-round. The Creature Conservancy came into being in 2005 due to an alligator named "Al." Al was abandoned on the steps of a local veterinary clinic. They called all around and could not find any group to adopt him...so they did.

Today, they house many different creatures from around the world. It includes a mix of rescue, transplant, and captive breeding guests. This is also an educational institution where guests learn that exotic pets are not a good idea. The staff here are all extremely knowledgeable about all the inhabitants.

Throughout the day, there are a number of demonstrations on a well-designed stage where guests can get an up-close view of many of these animals. Keepers have been handling and training most of the creatures here to help keep a safe environment for animals and humans alike. These demonstrations provide a lot of information about the animal species and how they came to be at the Conservancy.

DAYS AND HOURS OF OPERATION

The Creature Conservancy is open year-round, and some visits are by appointment only. They accommodate school field trips as well as personal tours, which can be found on their website.

MUST SEE

For most of my research, I chose to enter the various parks as a general admission guest. Since this visit was planned during February, I decided to pay extra for a private tour of the facility. The private tour is my "Must See" for this chapter.

Once I announced myself at the gate and showed my online receipt, I was greeted by the General Manager, who is a young woman that wears many hats here. They were getting ready for their African porcupine demonstration and our guide was also working with these animals on stage. She guided us to the seating area that stretched along this long stage. During this session, we learned all about this species of porcupine. Immediately after the demonstration, she returned this prickly rodent back to its enclosure, came back and found me, and began our tour.

117

The private tour consisted of entering many enclosures for personal meet and greet opportunities. I was allowed to scratch the neck of Emma, the resident aldabra giant tortoise. She likes getting her neck scratched and responds by extending her head from her shell. Then, I was able to meet Tulip, who is a red kangaroo and the model for their logo. She was very friendly and welcomed us to feel the fur on her back.

Then, my tour was temporarily halted, as our guide had to prepare for an educational session with their female cougar. Remember my comment about her wearing many hats? However, the neat thing about this deviation was that I was invited to help prepare for this session by hiding food around the enclosure. It was interesting having a large group of people watching as I placed and hid morsels of raw meat and other food. Once we all cleared the enclosure and the door was locked, they released this young cougar back into her enclosure. Due to the size of the habitat, she cannot adequately hunt with her sense of sight. Nevertheless, she did make quick work with her sense of smell and found all of her specially formulated treats.

I will not describe my every animal encounter, but I will wrap up with a very personal and pleasing meet-and-greet with a pair of two-toed sloths. I had the opportunity to feed them grapes using a straw so as not to get too close to their small but powerful jaws. I was invited to touch their fur for a very interesting experience. To end the tour, I even got to peek at a baby sloth that was born on the property.

So, my final comment is that if you can fit this private tour into your budget, I highly recommend it. You will not be disappointed!

FIELD NOTES

When walking into each building, take a moment, and look up at the ceiling. You might find a furry surprise or two.

If you visit during the warmer months, a number of demonstrations are held outside including, one with Al.

This is an educational facility, and many of the creatures living here were either hand-raised by people as pets or were injured and therefore cannot be released back into the wild. They have varying themes each week, month, and year. They designed their themes to focus on different animals to encourage return visits from their guests. Smart idea!

Find out why parrots and turtles are not necessarily the best animals to have as pets.

Ask any of the keepers which creatures are trained to interact with them and how they are trained. These folks hold all sorts of knowledge about these animals, and they love to share.

Their white alligator has a couple of unique talents. If not on the schedule for demonstration, be sure to ask any one of the expert keepers what those talents are. You will find it interesting.

CONTACT INFORMATION

The Creature Conservancy
4950 Ann Arbor Saline Rd
Ann Arbor, MI 48103
(734) 929-9324
Website:
http://www.thecreatureconservancy.org/
info@thecreatureconservancy.org

㉒ Wilderness Trails Zoo

TOWN

Birch Run

DESCRIPTION AND EXPERIENCE

At first, I thought that I had just paid to walk through a roadside micro-zoo. The first exhibit guided me through a number of roomy enclosures of macaws and other exotic birds. Initially, that is all I saw. A few minutes later, however, I discovered that there was much more to this gem of a zoo.

The Wilderness Trails Zoo opened to the public in 1991 and it spans across fifty-six acres. In 2003, the owners formed a non-profit and donated the entire animal collection to it. This zoo houses a large number of animals spanning over fifty different species.

From the main path, I took the first walkway to the right and it led me down to several large exhibits of herbivorous and carnivorous animals. Of course, they were not all mixed together; otherwise, it could get a little ugly.

The path ended between a rather large bobcat and an otter sliding into a pool. A turn left took me past a number of deep enclosures that are home to large herbivores such as American bison, zebra, deer, and others.

Down a little further was a small turn to my left that landed me into what ended up being one of my favorite places in the park. It was decorated like an old western ghost town with antiques and such on display. Amongst these icons from times past rested many types of reptile. This was a reptile town. The amazing thing about this section is that the reptiles were all outside. Moreover, with it being a little warm outside, many creatures were actively moving about their spacious enclosures.

Near the end of the reptile town, I walked upon an interesting sight. A large tortoise was walking towards me, and it had a large can strapped onto its shell. He was soliciting donations to help with reptile rescue efforts. Well, the tortoise did not tell me this, but the gentleman with him did. Through our conversation, I learned that Mr. Niezgucki and his wife started the reptile rescue at the Wilderness Trails Zoo over twenty years ago and run it to this day. The highest number of rescues, he stated, were alligators and tortoises. In fact, they have rescued so many that they loan a number of reptiles out to other zoos.

So, walking back through to spend more time with the carnivores, I chanced to meet a young zookeeper that was preparing to feed their pair of black bears. She coaxed them into a smaller holding pen with very large carrots. When they were preoccupied with their treat, she reached up and pushed a small gate closed, where it automatically latched for her. This allowed her to walk into the pen and secure that gate with a padlock. Once secure, she emptied two pails of goodies throughout the enclosure to encourage these bears to forage. There were carrots, sweet potatoes, avocado, and regular dry dog food. After that, she prepared the gates, so she could safely leave the pen while letting the bears back in to forage and enjoy their meal.

DAYS AND HOURS OF OPERATION

The Wilderness Trails Zoo is open between May and October.

MUST SEE

Easily, the reptile town and the Rainforest Experience building were the most interesting to me. Though I am not a huge reptile fan, it was pleasing to see exhibits that were not limited to glassed-in enclosures. It definitely made for better picture taking.

It was fun watching the otter enjoy the water slide on this warm day. Though it was warm outside, many animals were active.

FIELD NOTES

If you see a zookeeper feeding their guests a variety of foods such as I experienced with the bears, ask them what types of foods the animal eats there. If their diet includes a variety of items, ask if the animal has a particular favorite. I learned through my encounter that one bear like carrots best, while the other was a big fan of sweet potatoes

I still find it interesting how the carnivore and herbivore enclosures seemed close together, but none of the creatures there acted with any concern about it.

Listen to the various sounds in the park. Sometimes you can hear unusual noises. If you can find the source, you might be surprised that an animal can be so boisterous. I was taken aback when I heard a pair of coatimundi arguing. They were loud!

CONTACT INFORMATION

Wilderness Trails Zoo
11721 Gera Road (M-83)
Birch Run, MI 48415
(989) 624-6177
Website: http://wildernesstrailszoo.org/
wtzoo@hotmail.com

Zoo Tip:

Some zoos offer hands-on encounters. These are worth the potential wait in line.

㉓ Adventure Awaits

Please note that I have included all of the various zoos I discovered while researching this book. I am certain that I may have excluded an establishment or two. Feel free to recommend a Michigan-based zoo or wild animal park for inclusion in the next edition of this book.

TIPS FOR SUCCESS IN PLANNING YOUR ZOO ADVENTURE OR ZOOMARATHON:

Before heading out the door to visit one or more of the zoos mentioned in this book, do yourself a favor and go to their website first.

I would hate to hear that you drove two or more hours to discover that the zoo is closed to the public for one reason or another. So, keeping this mind, I have included a list of things to consider.

- Many zoos offer a discount if you pre-purchase tickets online. They may also offer group rates.

- Most zoos offer free entry for infants and toddlers, as well as discounts for veterans and the elderly.

- A large number of zoos depend on entry fees to pay their operational expenses. To increase their revenues, some establishments offer what I call "Add-on Adventures." These add-ons offer unique opportunities to experience the zoo and its inhabitants.

- Dress appropriately for the time of year and weather conditions of your visit. It can be fun watching animals interact in a rain shower, but not if you are not wearing a rain jacket or have an umbrella.

- Use the Map on the first pages of this book to see if any zoos are close enough that you can create a zoomarathon of two or more properties. It can make for a busy, but fun, adventure.

- If you like to map out your routes, Google Maps offers a feature where you can create directions to your destinations and then have them texted to your smartphone.

- Budget your trip:
  - Cost to get yourself or family through the gate.
  - Meals. If you have been to an amusement park, your meal budget should closely mirror that experience. If you have not been to an amusement park, consider a fast food restaurant, but at about two-to-three times the price. Many zoos allow you to bring a picnic meal, but please verify that before you go with that option.
  - Add-on adventures.
  - Gift store to get a replica of your favorite animal or other zoo-related treasures.
  - Batteries or a way to recharge your phone or camera for taking that perfect picture or selfie.

TIPS FOR SUCCESS ONCE YOU GET THROUGH THE FRONT GATES:

- Remember, it is all about the learning experience.
- Look for a schedule of the day's events. It should be posted near the entrance.
- Plan to attend as many wildlife demonstrations as you can fit in. Think of these as "free" encounters.
- Ask questions. Zookeepers and staff love talking about the animals and the zoo. All you have to do is ask them. Example questions may include:
  - How long have you been working here?
  - What animals do you care for?
  - Do the animals you care for have babies born in the park?
  - What is your favorite thing about working here?
  - What is your favorite animal here and why?

Finally, take a gazillion pictures! Well, as many as your battery or memory card will allow.

In closing, please respect the zoos you visit. Respect the animals you are viewing. Respect the keepers and the hard work they do keeping animals healthy and safe. Respect and assist those around you that might need assistance in some way.

Have a great time, and feel free to share your adventures with me as I have shared my adventures with you.

Never the end.

*9 7 8 1 7 3 3 8 9 1 6 0 8 *